KABBALAH
for BEGINNERS

A Beginner's Guide to
The Hidden Wisdom

KABBALAH
for BEGINNERS

A Beginner's Guide to
The Hidden Wisdom

BY
RABBI MICHAEL LAITMAN

COMPILED BY BENZION GIERTZ

LAITMAN
Kabbalah
Publishers

Executive Editor: Benzion Giertz

Laitman Kabbalah Publishers Website:
http://kabbalah.info
Laitman Kabbalah Publishers Email:
info@kabbalah.info

ISBN: 0-9732315-3-X
Second printing: January 2003

Contents

About the Book

The Kabbalist Rabbi Laitman, who was the student and personal assistant to Rabbi Baruch Ashlag from 1979-1991, follows in the footsteps of his rabbi in passing on the wisdom of Kabbalah to the world. This book is based on sources that were passed down by Rabbi Baruch's father, Rabbi Yehuda Ashlag (Baal HaSulam), the author of "the Sulam," the commentaries on The Book of Zohar, who continued the ways of the Ari and Rabbi Shimon Bar Yochai and many great Kabbalists throughout the generations before them.

The goal of this book is to assist individuals in confronting the first stages of the spiritual realm. This unique method of study, which encourages sharing this wisdom with others, not only helps overcome the trials and tribulations of everyday life, but initiates a process in which individuals extend themselves beyond the standard limitations of today's world.

Benzion Giertz
Executive Editor

Introduction

The laws of nature, our place in the world and our behavior have been studied by scientists and philosophers for thousands of years.

Along with logical assumptions, science uses quantifiable research and data. Yet our scientists and researchers have discovered that the more they advance in their research, the more obscure and confusing they find the world to be.

Science has undoubtedly brought enormous progress into the world, yet it is limited. Scientific tools cannot measure man's inner world, his soul, behavior and sources of motivation. Man, the major component of the creation, is still left without knowledge about his role in this universe.

Man has always looked for answers to the basic questions of life: Who am I? What is the purpose of my being here? Why does the world exist? Do we continue to exist after our physical being has completed its tasks?

In this world of constant pressure, some find temporary satisfaction in Eastern techniques, measures aimed at relaxation, or reducing suffering by minimizing personal expectations and desires. Various forms of meditation, nutrition, and physical and mental exercise quiet man's natural instincts and enable him to feel more comfortable from the point of view of his physical state. This process teaches him to lower his expectations, yet leaves him in conflict with his true desires.

Our life experience teaches us that we have unlimited desires—and only limited resources to satisfy them. This is the primary reason there is no way to completely satisfy all our desires and therefore avoid suffering. That is the subject of Kabbalah. Kabbalah answers the basic questions of life and guides us toward achieving unlimited satisfaction on a daily basis.

The essential questions of man's being add another dimension to human suffering. They do not allow us to feel satisfied even when this or that goal has been fulfilled. When one attains the goal he strives for, he immediately feels he's missing yet another pleasure. This prevents him from enjoying his achievements, and his suffering is renewed. In retrospect, he sees that he has spent most of his time making an effort to achieve his goals, and has gained very little pleasure from the successes themselves.

Everyone, each in his own way, tries to answer these questions from the sources of information at his disposal. Each one of us formulates our own perception of the world based on our experience. Reality and everyday life constantly put this perception to the test, making us react, improve, or otherwise change it. With some of us, this process occurs on a conscious level; with others it happens unconsciously.

Kabbalah reaches out to all those who are seeking awareness. It teaches you how to add an essential feeling of the spiritual sphere—the sixth sense—that will affect your life in this world. This will allow you to perceive the upper world—the Creator—and to gain control over your life.

The Bible, The Zohar, The Tree of Life and other authentic spiritual sources were set down in order to teach us how to progress in the spiritual realms, to study them and to receive spiritual knowledge. They explain how to set out on a path to spiritual ascent in this world. Over the generations, Kabbalists have written many books in various styles, each in accordance with the era in which they lived.

In total, four languages were created to introduce us to our spiritual reality: the language of the Bible (which includes the Five Books of Moses, the Prophets and the Scriptures), the language of legends, a legalistic language, and the language of Kabbalah, which describes the spiritual upper-worlds system and how to reach it. The differences in languages simply present various perspectives on the same subject in different formats—each suiting the generation it was intended for.

The Kabbalist Baal HaSulam writes in his book Fruits of the Wise:

> The inner wisdom of Kabbalah is the same as that of the Bible, The Zohar and the legends, with the only difference between them being the manner of the logic. It is rather like an ancient tongue translated into four languages. It is self-evident that the wisdom itself did not change at all due to the change in language. All we need to consider is which is most convenient and widely accepted for conveyance.

By reading this book, you will be able to take your first steps in understanding the roots of human behavior and the laws of nature. The contents present the essential principles of the Kabbalistic approach and describe the wisdom of Kabbalah and the way it works. *Kabbalah for Beginners* is intended for those searching for a sensible and reliable method of studying the phenomena of our world, for those seeking to understand the reasons for suffering and pleasure, for those seeking answers to the major questions of life.

Chapter 1

What is Kabbalah?

Kabbalah is an accurate method to investigate and define man's position in the universe. The wisdom of Kabbalah tells us the reason why man exists, why he is born, why he lives, what the purpose of his life is, where he comes from and where he is going after he completes his life in this world.

Kabbalah is a method of reaching the spiritual world. It teaches us about the spiritual world, and by studying it, we develop another sense. With the help of this sense we can be in touch with the upper worlds.

Kabbalah is not a theoretical study, but a very practical one. Man learns about himself, who he is, what he is like. He learns what he needs to do to change himself stage by stage and step by step. He conducts his research through his inner self.

All experimentation is conducted on himself, within himself. That is why Kabbalah is called "The Hidden Wisdom." Through Kabbalah a person undergoes internal changes that only he feels and knows are taking place. This activity occurs within a person; it is unique to him, and only he knows about it.

The word Kabbalah comes from the Hebrew word *lekabbel*, to receive. Kabbalah describes the motives of actions as "the desire to receive." This desire refers to receiving various kinds of pleasure. In order to receive pleasure, a person is usually willing to invest great effort. The question is, how can one attain the maximum amount of pleasure while paying a minimum price for it? Everyone tries to answer this question in his own way.

There is a certain order to the way the desire to receive develops and grows. In the first stage, man lusts after physical pleasure. Then he seeks money and honor. An even stronger desire makes him thirst for power. He may later develop a desire for spirituality, which is at the peak of the pyramid. A person who recognizes how great his desire for spirituality begins to seek ways of satisfying this desire.

The passage through the stages of the desire to receive makes a person become familiar with his abilities and limitations.

Kabbalah deals with the upper worlds, the roots of our feelings and thoughts, which we cannot grasp. Since we have no control over the worlds, we do not know how and why our feelings and thoughts are created. We wonder at experiences such as sweet, bitter, pleasant, rough and so forth. We are unsuccessful at building scientific tools to examine our feelings, even in the field of psychology, psychiatry and other social disciplines. Behavioral factors remain hidden from our understanding.

Kabbalah is a system for scientifically evaluating our feelings: It takes the total of our feelings and desires, and provides an exact scientific formula for each and every phenomenon, at each level, for every type of understanding and feeling.

This is the work of feelings combined with intellect. It uses, for beginning students, geometry, matrices and diagrams. When studying Kabbalah, they recognize each of their own feelings and begin to understand it. They know what name it should be given according to its power, direction and character.

The wisdom of Kabbalah is an ancient and proven method. Through it, man can receive higher awareness and attain spirituality. This is really his goal in this world. When a person feels a desire for spirituality, he starts to feel a longing for it, and can then develop the desire through the wisdom of Kabbalah that has been provided by the Creator.

Kabbalah is a word that describes the aim of the Kabbalist: to attain everything man is capable of, as a thinking being, the highest of all creatures.

Chapter 2

Why Study Kabbalah?

When an ordinary person studies the writings of the Kabbalists, he learns about what was formerly hidden from him. Only after acquiring the sixth sense through study does he begin to feel and see what was previously unrevealed.

Everyone has a natural ability to develop this sixth sense, and that is the reason Kabbalists transmit their knowledge of the structure of the upper, spiritual world. [See the chapter on "Sensing Reality through Kabbalah."]

When a person is exposed to Kabbalistic materials, he may not at first grasp what he is reading. But if he wants to understand, and tries to do so in the proper manner, he invokes what is called the Surrounding Light, the light that corrects him; and very gradually he is shown his spiritual reality. The terms "to correct" and "correction" are used in Kabbalah to describe a change in the desire to receive, i.e., to acquire the qualities of the spiritual world and of the Creator.

Everyone has this sixth, still-dormant spiritual sense; this is called the point of the heart. Opposite it stands the light, which will eventually fill the point, the sixth sense, when it develops.

The sixth sense is also called the spiritual Vessel (*Kli*), and it continues to exist even without material reality. The spiritual Vessel of the ordinary person who has never studied Kabbalah is not sufficiently developed to feel the spiritual world. When he studies the original Kabbalah writings in the proper way, this light enlightens the point of the heart and begins to develop it. The point then begins to widen and it expands sufficiently to allow the Surrounding Light to enter it. When the light enters into the point of the heart, it gives a person a spiritual feeling. This point is the person's soul.

Nothing is possible without help from the upper world, without the Surrounding Light descending from above and gradually lighting the way for a person. Even when we do not recognize this light, there is a direct connection between the point of the heart and the light due to fill it, as planned from above. Studying Kabbalah books enables a person to connect to the source of the light, and gradually come to feel a desire for spirituality. This process is called *segula* (remedy).

Rabbi Yehuda Ashlag wrote in the Introduction to the Study of the Ten Sefirot:

> Accordingly, why did the Kabbalists instruct everyone to study Kabbalah? While it is great and worthwhile publicizing that there is an incomparably wonderful quality to studying Kabbalah wisdom, even though they do not know what they are studying, it is the tremendous desire to understand what they are studying that awakens the lights surrounding their soul. That means that every person is assured the possibility of eventually attaining all the wonderful achievements the Creator intended for us in planning Creation.

> Those who do not attain them in this incarnation will do so in another, until the Creator's intention is fulfilled. Even if a person does not achieve this completion, the lights are destined to be his; the Surrounding Lights wait for him to prepare his Vessel to receive them. Therefore, even when he lacks the Vessels, when a person is engaged in this wisdom and recalls the names of the lights and Vessels waiting and belonging to him, they will shine on him but only to a certain degree. But they will not penetrate his inner soul, since his Vessels are not yet

ready to accept them. Kabbalah is the only means to create the Vessel to receive the light of the Creator. The light he receives when he is engaged in the wisdom imparts to him a grace from above, bestowing an abundance of holiness and purity on him, bringing him closer to reaching completion.

Kabbalah is special in that it gives a person a taste of spirituality while he is studying, and from that experience he comes to prefer spirituality to materialism. In proportion to his spirituality, he clarifies his will and learns to distance himself from things he was once attracted to, much as an adult is no longer attracted to childish games.

Why do we need Kabbalah? Because Kabbalah is given to us as a springboard for change. It is given to us so that we can know and perceive the Creator at any given moment throughout the day. These are the only reasons why the wisdom of Kabbalah was provided. Whoever learns Kabbalah in order to alter himself and improve himself, in order to know the Creator, reaches the stage in which he begins to see he can improve, and fulfill his true destiny in this lifetime.

Chapter 3

Who is a Kabbalist?

The Kabbalist is a researcher who studies his nature using a proven, time-tested and accurate method. He studies the essence of his existence using tools we can all utilize—feelings, intellect and heart.

A Kabbalist looks like an ordinary person. He need not have any special skills, talents, or occupation. He need not be a wise man or wear a holy expression. At some point in his life, this ordinary person decided to look for a way in which he would find credible answers to the questions that were troubling him. By utilizing a distinct method of learning, he was successful in acquiring an extra sense—a sixth sense—which is the spiritual sense.

Through this sense, the Kabbalist feels the spiritual spheres as a clear reality, just as we feel our reality here; he receives knowledge about the spiritual spheres, the upper worlds, and the revelation of higher forces. These worlds are called upper worlds, since they are higher than and beyond our world.

The Kabbalist ascends from his current spiritual level to the next one. This movement brings him from one upper world to the next. He sees the roots from which everything that exists here has developed, everything that fills our world, including ourselves. The Kabbalist is simultaneously in our world, and in the upper worlds. This quality is shared by all Kabbalists.

Kabbalists receive the real information that surrounds us, and feel this reality. Therefore, they can study it, be familiar with it, and teach us about it. They provide a new method through which we can meet the source of our lives, leading us to spirituality. They use books that are written in a special language. We must read these books in a special way, so they become a Vessel for discovering the truth for us as well.

In the books they have written, the Kabbalists inform us about the techniques based on man's personal experiences. From their all-encompassing point of view, they have found the way to help those who would follow, and then climb the same ladder as they did. Their method is called the wisdom of Kabbalah.

Chapter 4

The History of Kabbalah and The Zohar

The first Kabbalist we know of was the patriarch Abraham. He saw the wonders of human existence, asked questions of the Creator, and the upper worlds were revealed to him. The knowledge he acquired, and the method used in its acquisition, he passed on to coming generations. Kabbalah was passed among the Kabbalists from mouth to mouth for many centuries. Each Kabbalist added his unique experience and personality to this body of accumulated knowledge. Their spiritual achievements were described in the language relevant to the souls of their generation.

Kabbalah continued to develop after the Bible (the Five Books of Moses) was written. In the period between the First and Second Temples (586 BCE — 515 BCE), it was already being studied in groups. Following the destruction of the Second Temple (70 CE) and until the current generation, there have been three particularly important periods in the development of Kabbalah, during which the most important writings on Kabbalah study methods were issued.

The first period occurred during the 2nd century, when the book of The Zohar was written by Rabbi Shimon Bar Yochai, "the Rashbi." This was around the year 150 CE. Rabbi Shimon was a pupil of the famous Rabbi Akiva (40 CE — 135 CE). Rabbi Akiva and several of his disciples were tortured and killed by the Romans, who felt threatened by his teaching of the Kabbalah. They flayed his skin and stripped his bones with an iron scraper (like today's currycomb) for cleaning their horses. Following the death of 24,000 of Rabbi Akiva's disciples, the Rashbi was authorized by Rabbi Akiva and Rabbi Yehuda Ben Baba to teach future generations the Kabbalah as it had been taught to him. Rabbi Shimon Bar Yochai and four others were the only ones to survive. Following the capture and imprisonment of Rabbi Akiva, the Rashbi escaped with his son, Elazar. They hid in a cave for 13 years.

They emerged from the cave with The Zohar, and with a crystallized method for studying Kabbalah and achieving spirituality. The Rashbi reached the 125 levels man can achieve during his life in this world. The Zohar tells us that he and his son reached the level called "Eliyahu the Prophet," meaning that the Prophet himself came to teach them.

The Zohar is written in a unique form; it is in the form of parables and is presented in Aramaic, a language spoken in biblical times. The Zohar tells us that Aramaic is "the reverse side of Hebrew," the hidden side of Hebrew. Rabbi Shimon Bar Yochai did not write this himself; he conveyed the wisdom and the way to reach it in an organized manner by dictating its contents to Rabbi Aba. Aba rewrote The Zohar in such a way that only those who are worthy of understanding would be able to do so.

The Zohar explains that human development is divided into 6,000 years, during which time souls undergo a continuous process of development in each generation. At the end of the process souls reach a position of "the end of correction," i.e., the highest level of spirituality and wholeness.

Rabbi Shimon Bar Yochai was one of the greatest of his generation. He wrote and interpreted many Kabbalistic subjects that were published and are well known to this day.

On the other hand, the book of The Zohar, disappeared after it was written.

According to legend, The Zohar writings were kept hidden in a cave in the vicinity of Safed in Israel. They were found several hundred years later by Arabs residing in the area. A Kabbalist from Safed purchased some fish at the market one day, and was astonished to discover the priceless value of the paper in which they had been wrapped. He immediately set about purchasing the remaining pieces of paper from the Arabs, and collected them into a book.

This happened because the nature of hidden things is such that they must be discovered at a suitable moment, when suitable souls reincarnate and enter into our world. That is how The Zohar came to be revealed over time.

The study of these writings was conducted in secret by small groups of Kabbalists. The first publication of this book was by Rabbi Moshe de Leon, in the 13th century in Spain.

The second period of the development of Kabbalah is very important to the Kabbalah of our generation. This is the period of "the Ari," Rabbi Yitzhak Luria, who created the transition between the two methods of Kabbalah study. The first time the pure language of Kabbalah appeared was in the writings of the Ari. The Ari proclaimed the start of a period of open mass study of Kabbalah.

The Ari was born in Jerusalem in 1534. A child when his father died, his mother took him to Egypt where he grew up in his uncle's home.

During his life in Egypt, he made his living in commerce but devoted most of his time to studying Kabbalah. Legend has it that he spent seven years in isolation on the island of Roda on the Nile where he studied The Zohar, books by the first Kabbalists, and writings by another rabbi of his generation, "the Ramak," Rabbi Moshe Cordovero.

In 1570, the Ari arrived in Safed, Israel. Despite his youth, he immediately started teaching Kabbalah. His greatness was soon recognized; all the wise men of Safed, who were very knowledgeable in the hidden and revealed Wisdom, came to study with him, and he became famous. For a year-and-a-half his disciple Rabbi Chaim Vital committed to paper the answers to many of the questions that arose during his studies.

The Ari left behind a basic system for studying Kabbalah, which is still in use today. Some of these writings are *Etz Hachayim* (The Tree of Life), *Sha'ar HaKavanot* (The Gateway of Intentions), *Sha'ar HaGilgulim* (The Gateway of Reincarnation), and others. The Ari died in 1572, still a young man. His writings were archived according to his last wish, in order not to reveal his doctrine before the time was ripe.

The great Kabbalists provided the method and taught it, but knew that their generation was still unable to appreciate its dynamics. Therefore, they often preferred to hide or even burn their writings. We know that Baal HaSulam burned and destroyed a major part of his writings. There is special significance in this fact that the knowledge was committed to paper, and later destroyed. Whatever is revealed in the material world affects the future, and is revealed easier the second time.

Rabbi Vital ordered other parts of the Ari's writings to be hidden and buried with him. A portion was handed down to his son, who arranged the famous writings, The Eight Gates. Much later, a group of scholars headed by Rabbi Vital's grandson removed another portion from the grave.

Study of The Zohar in groups started openly only during the period of the Ari. The study of The Zohar then prospered for two hundred years. In the great Hassidut period (1750 — to the end of the 19th century), almost every great rabbi was a Kabbalist. Kabbalists appeared, mainly in Poland, Russia,

Morocco, Iraq, Yemen and several other countries. Then, at the beginning of the 20th century, interest in Kabbalah waned until it almost completely disappeared.

The third period of the development of Kabbalah contains an additional method to the Ari's doctrines, written in this generation by Rabbi Yehuda Ashlag, who authored the commentary of the *Sulam* (ladder) of The Zohar, and the Ari's teachings. His method is particularly suited to the souls of the current generation.

Rabbi Yehuda Ashlag is known as "Baal HaSulam" for his rendition of the Sulam of The Zohar. Born in 1885 in Lodz, Poland, he absorbed a deep knowledge of the written and oral law in his youth, and later became a judge and teacher in Warsaw. In 1921, he immigrated to Israel with his family and became the rabbi of Givat Shaul in Jerusalem. He was already immersed in writing his own doctrine when he began to pen the commentary of The Zohar in 1943. Baal HaSulam finished writing his commentary of The Zohar in 1953. He died the following year and was buried in Jerusalem at the Givat Shaul cemetery.

His eldest son, Rabbi Baruch Shalom Ashlag, "the Rabash," became his successor. His books are structured according to his father's instructions. They gracefully elaborate on his father's writings, facilitating our comprehension of his father's commentaries as handed down to our generation.

The Rabash was born in Warsaw in 1907 and immigrated to Israel with his father. Only after Rabbi Baruch was married did his father include him in study groups of selected students learning the hidden wisdom of Kabbalah. He was soon allowed to teach his father's new students.

Following his father's death, he took it upon himself to continue teaching the special method he had learned. Despite his great achievements, like his father, he insisted on keeping to a very modest way of life. During his lifetime he worked as a cobbler, construction worker and clerk. Externally, he lived like any ordinary person, but devoted every spare moment to studying and teaching Kabbalah. The Rabash died in 1991.

Rabbi Yehuda Ashlag, the Baal HaSulam, is the recognized spiritual leader for our generation. He is the only one in this generation who has written a fully comprehensive and updated commentary of The Zohar and the writings of the Ari. These books, with the addition of his son Rabbi Baruch Ashlag's essays, are the only source we can use to assist us in further progress.

When we study their books, we are actually studying The Zohar and the Ari's writings through the most recent commentaries (of the past 50 years). This is a life belt for our generation, since it enables us to study ancient texts as if they had been written now, and to use them as a springboard to spirituality.

Baal HaSulam's method suits everyone, and the *sulam* (ladder) he built in his writings ensures that none of us need fear studying Kabbalah. Anyone learning Kabbalah is assured that within three to five years he will be able to reach spiritual spheres, all realities and divine understanding, which is the name given to that which is above and beyond us and not yet felt by us. If we study according to the books of Rabbi Yehuda Ashlag, the Baal HaSulam, we can reach true correction.

The study method is constructed to awaken in us a desire to understand the upper worlds. We are given a greater desire to get to know our roots and to connect with them. We are then empowered to improve and fulfill ourselves.

All three great Kabbalists are of the same soul: first appearing as Rabbi Shimon, on a second occasion as the Ari, and the third time as Rabbi Yehuda Ashlag. On each occasion, the timing was ripe for further revelation because the people of that generation were worthy, and the soul descended to teach the method suitable for that generation.

Each generation is increasingly worthy of discovering The Zohar. What was written by Rabbi Shimon Bar Yochai and hidden was later discovered by the generation of Rabbi Moshe de Leon, and then by the Ari, who started to interpret it in the language of Kabbalah. These writings were also stored away and partly rediscovered when the timing was right. Our generation is privileged to learn from the Sulam, which enables everyone to study Kabbalah and to correct himself now.

We see that The Zohar speaks to each generation. In each generation it is more revealed and better understood than in the generation before. Each generation opens the book of The Zohar in a unique way, suited to the roots of its particular soul.

Importantly, at the same time, an attempt is made to conceal Kabbalistic writings so that those feeling the need to seek them will discover them by themselves. The Kabbalists evidently know that the process of change requires two conditions: correct timing and maturity of the soul. We are witnessing a very interesting occurrence, characterized by the breakthrough and signaling of a new era in the study of Kabbalah.

Chapter 5

Who Can Study Kabbalah?

Whenever Kabbalah is discussed, statements are tossed about such as: One can go mad studying Kabbalah; it is safe to study Kabbalah only after the age of 40; a man must be married and have at least three children before embarking on its study; women are forbidden to study Kabbalah, etc.

Kabbalah is open to all. It is for those who truly wish to correct themselves in order to attain spirituality. The need comes from the soul's urge to correct itself. That is actually the only test to determine whether a person is ready to study Kabbalah: the desire to correct oneself. This desire must be genuine and free of outside pressure, since only one's self can discover one's true desire.

The great Kabbalist, the Ari, wrote that from his generation onwards Kabbalah was intended for men, women and children, and that all could and should study Kabbalah. The greatest Kabbalist in our generation, Yehuda Ashlag, Baal HaSulam, left a new study method for this generation. It is suitable for anyone wishing to embark on the study of Kabbalah.

A person finds his way to Kabbalah when he is no longer satisfied by material reward and hopes studying will provide answers, clarification and new opportunities. He no longer finds solutions in this world to the significant questions concerning his existence. More often than not, the hope of finding answers is not even cognitive; he simply takes an interest and finds it necessary.

Such a person has questions: Who am I? Why was I born? Where do I come from? Where am I going? Why do I exist in the world? Was I already here? Will I reappear? Why is there so much suffering in the world? Can it somehow be avoided? How can I attain pleasure, completeness, peace of mind? Unconsciously, he feels the answers to these questions can be found only beyond the realm of this world.

The one answer to these questions is to know and feel the upper worlds, and the way to do so is through Kabbalah. Through its wisdom, man enters the upper worlds with all his feelings. They are worlds that provide all of the reasons for his existence in this world. He takes control of his life, thereby attaining his goal—tranquility, pleasure and completeness—while he is still in this world.

In the Introduction to the Study of the Ten Sefirot it is written: "If we put our hearts into answering just one famous question, I am sure all questions and doubts will disappear from the horizon and we will find they are gone. And that tiny question is—What is the point of our lives?"

Anyone attracted to the study of Kabbalah due to this question is welcome to study Kabbalah. The one who reaches serious study feels this question and asks himself constantly: "What is the point of our lives?" This is what urges him to search and find answers.

People want quick cures. They want to learn about magic, meditation and healing associated with Kabbalah. They are not truly interested in the revelation of the upper worlds, or in learning the methods of reaching spiritual realms. This does not qualify as a genuine desire to study Kabbalah.

When the time is right and the need is there, a person will look for a framework of study and will not be satisfied until he finds one. Everything depends on the root of man's soul and that point of his heart. A true desire within his heart to discover and feel the upper worlds will lead him to the way of Kabbalah.

Chapter 6

How To Study Kabbalah

Several hundred years ago, it was impossible to find Kabbalah books or books on this subject. Kabbalah was transmitted solely from one Kabbalist to another, never reaching the ordinary person. Today, the situation is reversed. There is a desire to circulate the material among all, and to call on everyone to participate in its study. When studying these books, the desire for spirituality grows, whereby the light surrounding us, the real world hidden from us, starts to reflect on those people who wish to be closer to the special charm of spirituality, and they start to desire it even more.

Kabbalists prohibited the study of Kabbalah by people who had not been prepared for it, unless they did so under special circumstances. They treated their students cautiously to ensure they studied in the proper manner. They limited students by certain criteria.

Baal HaSulam describes these reasons at the beginning of his Introduction to the Study of the Ten Sefirot. However, if we understand these restrictions as conditions for the proper comprehension of Kabbalah, we will see that they are intended as a way to prevent students from deviating from the correct way.

What has changed is that we now have more of a language, better conditions and a stronger determination to study Kabbalah. Because souls feel the need to study Kabbalah, Kabbalists such as Baal HaSulam have written commentaries that enable us to study free of errors. Everyone can now learn Kabbalah through his books.

To study Kabbalah in the proper way, it is recommended that the student focus solely on the writings of the Ari, Baal HaSulam and Rabash in their original versions.

The primary objective of Kabbalah is to achieve spirituality.

Only one thing is necessary—proper instruction. If a person studies Kabbalah in the right way, he progresses without forcing himself. There can be no coercion in spirituality.

The aim of study is for a person to discover the connection between himself and what is written in the book; this should always be borne in mind. That is the reason Kabbalists wrote down what they experienced and achieved. It is not in order to acquire knowledge of how reality is built and functions, as in science. The intention of the Kabbalah texts is to create an understanding and assimilation of its spiritual truth.

If a person approaches the texts in order to gain spirituality, the text becomes a source of light and corrects him. If he approaches the texts in order to gain wisdom, it is for him mere wisdom. The measure of inner demand is what determines the measure of strength he gleans, and the pace of his correction.

That means that if a person studies in the proper manner, he crosses the barrier between this world and the spiritual world. He enters a place of inner revelation and reaches the light. That is known as the beautiful sign. If he does not achieve this, it is a sign that he has been negligent in the quality or quantity of his efforts; he did not make a sufficient effort. It is not a question of how much he studied, but a question of how focused he was on his intentions, or if he lacked something. However, if he reaches this desire to correct himself, he can attain spirituality. Only then will the heavens open for him to allow his entry into another world, another reality, another dimension. He reaches this stage by studying Kabbalah in the right way.

Embracing Kabbalah does not work by merely avoiding nice things so that one's desire will not be kindled. Correction does not come from self-punishment, but rather as a result of spiritual achievement. When a person achieves spirituality, the light appears and corrects him.

This is the only way a person changes. Any other way is hypocritical. He is mistaken if he believes that by putting on a nice appearance he will achieve spirituality. Inner correction will not follow, since only the light can correct. The purpose of studying is to invite the light that corrects one. Therefore, a person should work on himself only for that purpose.

If there is any pressure, or any obligatory rules or regulations, it is a sign that it is man-made and is not an action intended by the upper worlds. In addition, inner harmony and tranquility are not prerequisites for attaining spirituality; they will appear as a result of the correction. But a person should not believe this can happen without an effort on his part.

The Kabbalah way absolutely rejects any form of coercion. It grants a person an inkling of spirituality, bringing him to prefer it to materialism. Then, in relation to his spirituality, he clarifies his desire. Accordingly, he retreats from material things as his attraction to or necessity for them disappears.

Studying Kabbalah incorrectly, even with the best intentions, can distance a person from spirituality. This type of student will only fail.

Among the languages of the study of spiritual worlds, between the Bible (which includes the Five Books of Moses, the Prophets and the Scriptures) and Kabbalah, the latter is the most useful and direct. Those who learn it cannot err in their understanding. It does not use names from this world, but possesses a special dictionary directly indicating the spiritual tools for spiritual objects and forces, and the correlation between them.

It is therefore the most useful language for the student to make inner progress and to correct himself. If we study the writings of Baal HaSulam, there is no danger of becoming confused.

Spirituality can be attained by studying the right books, i.e., books written by a true Kabbalist. The Bible's texts are Kabbalah texts. They are books Kabbalists wrote to one another to exchange ideas and to assist each other in learning. A person whose spiritual feelings have grown can see how these books assist him in continuing his growth and development. It is like being led by a tour guide in a foreign country. With the aid of the guidebook, the traveler becomes oriented and better understands his new whereabouts.

We need books that are suited to our souls, books by the Kabbalists of our generation or the previous one, since different souls descend in each generation and require different teaching methods.

A student in search of a Kabbalah teacher must do so with care. There are so-called Kabbalists who teach incorrectly. For example, it is sometimes claimed that wherever the word "body" is written it refers to our physical body, that the right hand symbolizes charity and the left, bravery. This is exactly the strict prohibition rendered by the Bible and Kabbalists in "Thou shall not make a sculpture or a picture."

Why are there those who teach and interpret this way? First of all, they themselves do not comprehend the kabbalistic language of branches. [See the chapter on "The Language Of Kabbalists: Branches."] If there were a direct connection between spiritual forces and our physical bodies, it would have been possible to teach people to succeed in life, and to cure the body by physical means under the guise of spirituality.

It is important to join the right study group in which to explore the writings of a real Kabbalist. This should be done under the guidance of a Kabbalist.

The group provides strength. Everybody has at least a small desire for materialism, and an even smaller desire for spiritualism. The way to augment the will for spiritualism is through joint desire. Several students together stimulate *Ohr makif* (Surrounding Light). Although the physical body separates people, it does not affect spiritualism, since in spiritualism, the point of the heart is shared by all, resulting in a much greater result.

All of the Kabbalists studied in groups. Rabbi Shimon Bar Yochai held a group for students, and so did the Ari. A group is vital in order to progress. It is the primary tool of Kabbalah, and everyone is measured by his contribution to the group.

It is essential to receive from a true Kabbalist who himself studied under the guidance of a Kabbalist. A group does not eliminate the need for a Kabbalist; it is impossible without a Kabbalist since it is he who directs the group.

The texts and the Kabbalist help the student so that he does not deviate from the correct way of studying. He works on himself and on his inner being. No one knows the others' place in the group, nor his level of spirituality. The books, the group and the Kabbalist simply help him to stay on course and increase his will for spirituality, instead of following other desires or worthless endeavors.

To help students avoid failure, a list of questions and answers and an index of words and expressions is provided. During study sessions, attention is drawn to spiritual truth, not to the depth or measure of comprehension. What is important is that the student is motivated to make spiritual progress, and not merely to advance intellectually.

It is true that people are attracted to the wisdom of Kabbalah in the hope of becoming more successful. We are all made of the desire to receive pleasure. It is our basic makeup, but with proper instruction some of us attain spirituality and eternity. Others, without the proper instruction, live under the illusion that they have achieved something spiritual. In fact, they lose their chance of attaining spirituality in this lifetime.

Chapter 7

Spirituality and Kabbalah

Man is incapable of making a move without there being some advantage in it for him. In order to act, he must first see how he may gain from it. This gain serves as the fuel that gets him moving. The fuel is either the immediate or future gain he envisages. If a person does not feel there is any profit, he will immediately halt his actions. That is because man cannot exist without feeling he will gain something.

The Kabbalah teaches man *how* to receive. In order to attain spirituality a person must expand his will to receive. He must expand his will to absorb all worlds, including this one. This is the purpose for which he was created. It is not necessary to become a monk or ascetic, or steer away from life. On the contrary, Kabbalah obliges man to marry, bear children and work and live a full life. Nothing has to be given up; everything was created for a reason, and man need not withdraw from life.

When a person begins to study Kabbalah, he may have no spiritual feelings, and therefore he embarks on the learning process with the aid of his intellect. We are supposed to open our heart through our intellect. When the heart develops, we feel what is right and what is not, and are naturally drawn to the right decisions and actions.

The Kabbalists begin by teaching spirituality in small doses, to allow the students to expand their will to receive more light, more awareness, more spiritual feeling. Increased will brings with it a greater depth, understanding and attainment. A person then reaches the highest level of spirituality he can attain, to the roots of his soul.

Chapter 8

Reincarnation and Kabbalah

None of us are new souls; we all have accumulated experiences from previous lives in other incarnations. In each generation over the past six thousand years, souls have descended that were here on previous occasions. They are not new souls, but souls of a different kind that attained some form of spiritual development.

Souls descend to earth in a special order: They enter the world cyclically. The number of souls is not infinite; they return again and again, progressing toward correction. They are encased in new physical bodies that are more or less the same, but the types of souls that descend are different. This is referred to nowadays as reincarnation. Kabbalists use another term: the development of generations.

This intertwining, the connection of the soul and body, assists in the correction of the soul. Man is referred to as "soul," not "body." The body itself can be replaced, just as organs can now be replaced. The body is useful only in that it serves as an encasement through which the soul can work. Each generation physically resembles the previous one, but they are different from one another because each time the souls descend with the added experience of their previous lives here. They arrive with renewed strength obtained while they were in heaven.

Thus, each generation possesses different desires and goals from the previous one. This leads to the specific development of each generation. Even a generation that does not reach the desire to know true reality or God-like recognition accom-plishes the task by the suffering it endures. That is its way of making progress toward true reality.

All souls are derived from one, called *Adam HaRishon* (the soul of the First Man). This does not refer to Adam as a mere personality from the Bible. It is a concept of spiritual, inner reality. Parts of the soul of the first man descend into the world, taking the form of bodies, leading to a connec-tion between body and soul. Reality is directed in such a manner that the souls descend and correct themselves. When they enter into body form they raise their level 620 times above the level from which they began. The order in which souls descend into this reality of wearing a body goes from light to heavy.

The soul of the first man comprises many parts and many desires, some light, others heavy, based on the amount of egoism and cruelty they possess. They come into our world, the lighter ones first, the heavier ones following. Accordingly, correction requirements differ.

In their descent into the world, souls have gathered experience from their suffering. This is called the path of suffering, as this experience develops the soul. Each time it is reincarnated, it has an increased unconscious urge to seek answers to questions on its existence, its roots, and the importance of man's life.

Accordingly, there are souls that are less developed, and souls that are more so. The latter have such an enormous urge to recognize the truth that they cannot limit themselves to the confinements of this world. If they are given the right tools, the proper books and instruction, they will attain recognition of the spiritual world. Kabbalah also describes the descending souls as pure or as less refined. It is a measurement in direct proportion to how much the souls require for correction. Souls requiring a greater correction are called less refined.

As different souls descend, they require different guidance and correction, unique for that generation's souls. This is why in each generation there are people who lead us in our spiritual progress. They write books and form study groups in order to convey the method of discovery of the reality that is most suited to that generation. In this, the media age, they may appear on television, radio and most recently, on the Internet.

In the beginning (before the soul of Ari appeared), there was an era of experience gathering and perseverance in this world. The souls' existence was sufficient in order to make progress toward correction. The suffering they accumulated added urgency to their souls to relieve their suffering. The desire to leave their suffering behind was the motivating force behind the development of the generations.

That era continued until the 16th century, when the Ari appeared and wrote that from his generation onwards, men, women and children in all the nations of the world could, and were required to, engage in Kabbalah. The reason was that the time had arrived in the development of generations, in which souls descending into the world were able to recognize true reality and were ready to complete their correction by the special method the Ari had developed. They could achieve what was required of them.

Souls have but one desire—while existing within physical bodies—to return to their roots, to the level they were before their descent. Physical bodies, with their desire to receive, pull them back into this world. Man consciously wishes to rise spiritually. The great effort spent on the friction created by this dichotomy is what assists him in rising 620 times above his previous level.

If a soul does not complete its task, the next time it descends into the world, it will reincarnate more deserving of correction.

Sometimes, we believe that we should deny our desires and longing so that in the next reincarnation we will be more successful. We think we should not desire anything except a little nutrition and lying in the sun, as would a cat. However, the contrary is true since in the next round, we will be even more cruel, demanding, exacting and aggressive.

The Creator wants us to be filled with spiritual pleasure, to be complete. That is possible only through great desire. Only with a corrected desire can we truly reach the spiritual world and become strong and active. If our desire is small, while it cannot do great harm, it also cannot do much good. Desire is called corrected only when it functions out of the proper influence. It does not exist in us automatically, but is acquired while studying Kabbalah in the correct manner.

A pyramid of souls exists, based on the desire to receive. At the base of the pyramid are many souls with small desires, earthly, looking for a comfortable life in an animal-like manner: food, sex, sleep. The next layer comprises fewer souls, those with the urge to acquire wealth. These are people who are willing to invest their entire lives in making money, and who sacrifice themselves for the sake of being rich.

Next are those that will do anything to control others, to govern and reach positions of power. An even greater desire, felt by even fewer souls, is for knowledge; these are scientists and academics, who spend their lives engaged in discovering something specific. They are interested in nothing but their all-important discovery.

Located at the zenith of the pyramid is the strongest desire, developed by only a small few, for the attainment of the spiritual world. All these levels are built into the pyramid.

Man also has the same pyramid of desires within him, which he must overturn so that its sheer weight will compel him to aim for the purest desire, the infinite desire for truth. He must reject and discard all his earthly egoistic desires and put every effort and energy into increasing the desire for spirituality. He achieves this through the proper way of studying.

When a person truly wishes to increase his longing for spirituality, then the light around him, the spiritual world hidden from him, starts to reflect back on him, making him long for it even more. At this stage, group study under a Kabbalist's guidance is crucial. [See the chapter on "How To Study Kabbalah."]

A major change in the souls descending today lies in the fact that we are starting to see around us a definite desire to achieve a spiritual system. Even ordinary people are seeking something spiritual, something beyond our world.

Although this "spirituality" may include all sorts of shortcuts, magic tricks and esoteric teachings and groups promising answers to those who join them, nevertheless, it bespeaks of the search for a different reality. If a generation displays a stronger desire within the souls themselves, a new method, suited to these souls, will emerge.

In the last fifteen years there has been swift and active development in the descent of new souls. The desire of these souls is much stronger and more genuine. It is directed at achieving the real truth and nothing else.

When we truly comprehend how reality applies to us and how we are affected by it, we will cease doing that which is prohibited; we will insist on the right thing and we will do it. Then we will discover harmony between the real world and ourselves.

In the meantime, we unconsciously err, then realize we have erred. It may appear that there is no possibility of escape. That is why mankind finds itself more and more in a blind alley, mired in increasingly difficult dilemmas. We will discover that there is no alternative to recognizing the spiritual world of which we are a part. This recognition will lead us to a new situation in which we will consciously begin to act as one collective body, and not just as individuals.

All people are connected to one another in one soul, from one generation of souls to the next. We all possess collective responsibility. That is why the Kabbalist is regarded as "founder of the world." He influences the entire world, and the world influences him.

Chapter 9

The Language of
Kabbalists: Branches

When we think or feel something and wish to convey it to someone else so that he may feel it too, we use words. There is a general consensus in the use of words and their meanings; when we call something "sweet," the other person immediately understands what we mean since he imagines the same taste. Yet how closely does his conception of sweet match ours? How can we best communicate our feelings while still using words?

The feelings of Kabbalists are above our level. Nevertheless, they wish to convey to us their wonder at things that have no meaning for us. They do this through means taken from our world: often words, sometimes music notes, and on occasion, by other means.

Kabbalists write about their experiences and feelings in the upper worlds. They write about the higher forces and what they discover there. They write for other Kabbalists, since the interaction of studies between them is so essential and so fruitful. Their writings are then extended to those who haven't yet sensed spirituality, for those whose spirituality is still hidden.

Since there are no words in the spiritual world to describe their spiritual feelings, Kabbalists call these experiences branches, a word taken from our world. Therefore the language used in books on Kabbalah is called the language of branches. It is a language that borrows words from our world and uses them to identify spiritual experiences. Since everything in the spiritual world has an equivalent in the physical world, each root of the spiritual world has a name and the name of its branch. And because we cannot describe our feelings precisely and do not know how to measure or compare them, we use all kinds of auxiliary words to help.

Rabbi Yehuda Ashlag writes in his book *Talmud Esser HaSefirot* (Study of the Ten Sefirot, Part 1 Looking Inwards):

> ...the Kabbalists chose a special language that can be referred to as the "language of branches." Nothing takes place in this world that is not drawn from its roots in the spiritual world. On the contrary, everything in this world originates in the spiritual world and then descends into this world. The Kabbalists accordingly found a ready language by which they could easily convey their achievements to one another orally and in writing for future generations. They took the names of branches from the material world; each name is self-explanatory and indicates its upper root in the higher world system.

For every force and action in this world there is a force and action in the spiritual world that is its root. Each spiritual force correlates to only one force, its branch in the material world.

Of this direct correlation it is written, "There is nothing growing below that does not have an angel above urging it to grow." That is, there is nothing in our world that does not have a corresponding force in the spiritual world. Because of this direct correlation, and because spirituality does not contain names—just feelings and forces without the mantle of animal, mineral, vegetable, or speech—Kabbalists use names of branches in this world in order to define their spiritual roots by them. Baal HaSulam writes further:

With all the explanations, you will comprehend what sometimes appear in the Kabbalah books as strange terminology for the human spirit, particularly in the basic Kabbalah books, The Zohar and books by the Ari. The question arises, why did Kabbalists use such simple terminology to express these lofty ideas? The explanation is that no language in the world can reasonably be used, except for the special language of branches, based on the corresponding upper roots... It should not be surprising if strange expressions are sometimes used, since there is no choice in the matter. The matter of good cannot replace the matter of bad, and vice versa. We must always convey precisely the branch or incident showing the upper root as the occasion dictates. We must also elaborate until the exact definition is found.

In Kabbalah, the student repeats the main ideas of Kabbalistic wisdom: "place," "time," "movement," "lack," "body," "body parts" or "organs," "match," "kiss," "hug," etc., over and over again, until he feels within himself the right feeling for every idea.

A final word: It should be noted that there are some so-called instructors of Kabbalah who communicate erroneous interpretations to their students. The error stems from the fact that the Kabbalists wrote their books using the language of branches and used words from our world to express spiritual ideas. Those who do not understand the correct use of this language are mistaken. They teach that there is a connection between the body and the spiritual Vessel, for example, as if by physical actions a person is doing something spiritual. The branches are an integral part of Kabbalah and without their use, one is not learning true Kabbalah.

Chapter 10

Sensing Reality through Kabbalah

Everything we know about our world is based on man-made study. Every generation studies our world and conveys its knowledge to the following generation. Through it, each generation comprehends the sort of framework in which he should live, and what his position is in relation to other generations. In each era, mankind uses the world surrounding him.

The same process takes place in spiritualism. Every generation of Kabbalists from Abraham onwards studies and discovers the spiritual worlds. Just as in scientific research, they pass along the knowledge they have attained to future generations.

In this world we have a general sense, called the desire to receive, with five receptors, which are our five senses. When a person undergoes a correction, he attains the sixth sense, known as the spiritual sense. This sense enables him to feel the spiritual reality. It is not in the same category as the other five senses whatsoever.

Scientists, too, use only their five senses. Any instrument—precise, advanced, technical, mechanical or otherwise—we regard as "objective." But these instruments merely expand the limits of our senses so that we may hear, see, smell, taste and touch more intricately. Ultimately, it is man who examines, measures and assesses the results of research, through his five senses. Obviously, he cannot provide an exact, objective answer to what is accomplished by the senses. Kabbalah, the source of all wisdom, enables us to do this.

When starting to study reality, we discover that we cannot study or understand that which is beyond us since it is unknown and unrevealed to us. If we cannot see it or touch or taste it, we may question whether it really exists. Only Kabbalists, those who attain a higher abstract upper light beyond our senses, are able to comprehend our true reality.

Kabbalists tell us that beyond our senses there is only an abstract upper light, called the Creator. Imagine that we are in the middle of the ocean, within a sea of light. We can sense all kinds of feelings that seem to be incorporated into it, as far as our ability to comprehend allows us. We do not hear what is happening elsewhere. What we regard as hearing comes as the response of our eardrums to external stimuli. We do not know what is causing it. We simply know that our eardrum reacts from within us. We assess it internally and accept it as an external event. We do not know what is happening outside of ourselves; we merely comprehend the reaction of our senses to it.

As in the example of hearing, so it is with our other senses: sight, taste, touch and smell. That means that we can never exit our "box." Whatever we say about what is happening externally is in fact the picture we paint inside us. This restriction can never be overcome.

The study of Kabbalah can assist us in expanding the borders of our natural senses to achieve the sixth sense, through which we can become acquainted with the reality around and within us. This reality is the true reality. Through it, we will be able to experience the reaction of our senses externally. If we direct all of our five senses correctly, we will see the true picture of reality. We need merely to internalize the characteristics of the spiritual world.

It is like a radio that is able to tune into a certain wavelength. The wavelength exists outside of the radio, which receives and responds to it. This example applies to us, too. If we experience at least one tiny spark of the spiritual world, we will begin to feel it within ourselves.

During his development, the Kabbalist acquires more and more spiritual characteristics, thereby connecting to all the levels of the spiritual world, all built on the same principle. When a person studies Kabbalah, he begins to understand, to feel, to assess and work with all realities, both spiritual and material, without differentiating between them. The Kabbalist reaches the spiritual world while encased in his body in this world. He feels the two worlds without any border separating them.

Only when a person experiences this true reality can he see the reasons for what is happening to him here. He understands the consequences of his actions. He then begins to be practical for the first time, living, feeling everything and knowing what he should do with himself and his life.

Prior to this recognition he does not have the ability to know why he was born, who he is and the consequences of his actions. Everything is enclosed within the borders of the material world, and the way he enters it is also the way he leaves it.

In the meantime, we are all at the level called "This World." Our senses are equally limited; therefore, we are capable only of seeing the same picture. Baal HaSulam writes, *"All upper and lower worlds are included in man."* This is the key sentence for anyone interested in the wisdom of Kabbalah and living the reality around him. The reality around us includes upper worlds as well as this world; together, they are part of man.

For the time being, we understand this world through material, physical elements. However, we add several elements when we study, through which we discover additional elements. It allows us to see things we cannot see today.

At first our level is very low, as we are located diametrically opposite the level of the Creator. But then we start to rise from this level by correcting our desire. We then discover another reality surrounding us, although no change actually occurs. We change within ourselves, and following the change, become aware of other elements surrounding us. Later, these elements disappear and we feel everything is due solely to the Creator, the Almighty. The elements we begin to gradually discover are called worlds.

We should not try to imagine spiritual reality, but should sense it. Imagining it merely distances us from its reach. Kabbalists reach the upper worlds through their senses, just as we reach out to the material world. The worlds stand between us and the Creator, hiding Him from us. As Baal HaSulam writes, it is as if the worlds filter the light for us. We can then see reality surrounding us in a different way. In fact, we will discover that there is nothing between us and the Creator.

All these disturbances, these worlds between us, hide Him from us. They are masks placed on our senses. We do not see Him in his true form; we see only fractured elements. In Hebrew, the origin of the word *Olam* (world) is *"alama"* (concealing). Part of the light is transmitted, and part is hidden. The higher the world, the less hidden the Creator is.

Those in this world paint different pictures of reality differently. Logic dictates that reality should be uniform to everyone. Nevertheless, one hears one thing, another hears something else, one sees one thing, and another sees it differently.

Baal HaSulam illustrates this by using electricity as an example: We have in our homes an electric socket that contains abstract energy which cools, heats, creates a vacuum or pressure depending on the appliance using it, and on the ability of the appliance to utilize the electricity. Yet the energy has no form of its own, and remains abstract. The appliance reveals the potential found in the electricity.

We can say the same about the upper light, the Creator that has no form. Each person feels the Creator according to the level of his correction. At the beginning of his studies, a person can see only that his reality exists, and is unable to sense any higher force.

He gradually discovers, through using his senses, the true, expanded reality. At a more advanced stage, if he corrects all his senses according to the light around him, there will be no separation between himself and the light, between man and the Creator. It will be as if there is no difference between their characteristics. The person then achieves godliness in the real sense. Godliness is the highest level of spirituality.

How can a beginner master this science when he cannot even properly understand his teacher? The answer is very simple. It is only possible when we spiritually lift ourselves up above this world.

Only if we rid ourselves of all of the traces of material egoism and accept attaining spiritual values as our true goal. Only the longing and the passion for spirituality in our world—that is the key to the higher world.

Chapter 11

Kabbalistic Music

Rabbi Yehuda Ashlag (Baal HaSulam), author of the Sulam commentary of The Zohar, expressed his spiritual feelings through the words of his numerous published writings. Among them he wrote songs and composed melodies based on these spiritual feelings.

The music itself is based on the way a person feels in the spiritual world. What is so special about the music is that everyone can understand it, even if he has not reached the composer's spiritual level. Listening to the Baal HaSulam's music, as conveyed by his son Rabbi Baruch Ashlag, we have the opportunity to experience the spiritual sentiments of these prominent Kabbalists.

The Kabbalist achieves two polarized stages in spiritualism: agony, as a result of drifting away from the Creator, and delight, as a result of getting closer to Him. The feeling of drifting away from the Creator produces sad music, expressed by a prayer appealing for closeness. The feeling of closeness to the Creator produces joyous music, expressed by a thanksgiving prayer.

Therefore, we hear and feel two distinct moods in the music: longing and desire for unification when drifting away, and love and happiness when discovering unification. The two moods together express the Kabbalist's unification with the Creator.

The music bathes the listener in a wondrous light. We do not need to know anything about it before listening to it, since it is wordless. Yet its effect on our hearts is direct and swift. Hearing it over and over again is a special experience.

The notes are composed in adherence to Kabbalistic rules. The notes are chosen according to the way man's soul is built. The listener feels them penetrating deep within his soul, unobstructed. This happens because of the direct connection between our souls and the roots of the notes.

In 1996, 1998, and 2000, three CDs of the Baal HaSulam's and Rabash's music were recorded and published. The melodies are presented as Rabbi Michael Laitman heard them from his rabbi, Rabbi Baruch Ashlag, eldest son and follower of the ways of Baal HaSulam.

Chapter 12

FAQs About Kabbalah

We learn about Kabbalah by listening, reading, studying in groups and most importantly, asking questions and receiving answers. Following are some of the most frequently asked questions drawn from our Web site.

If you have any questions you would like us to answer, please write to info@kabbalah.info or visit our web site at www.kabbalah.info.

Q.1 **I have been asking myself about my place in the world. I don't know whether Kabbalah is for me. What is Kabbalah all about and what good will it do me if I study it?**

A.1 Kabbalah gives one answer to one common question: What is the essence of my life and my existence? Kabbalah is for those who have been searching for answers; these people are best suited to studying Kabbalah. Kabbalah shows man the source and thus, the purpose of his life.

Q.2 **I have always thought that Kabbalah is a secret. Suddenly, Kabbalah has become the new, hot topic. How did this happen?**

A.2 For thousands of years it was prohibited to disseminate Kabbalah. Only during the 20th century, when the books of the Kabbalist Rabbi Yehuda Ashlag were published, have we been afforded the possibility of studying Kabbalah without restrictions. His writings are aimed at helping people like you, those without previous knowledge of Kabbalah. It is permissible to distribute Kabbalah widely and to teach everyone who is seeking the missing spiritual elements in his life.

Q.3 **Is it true that Rabbi Ashlag thought that Kabbalah should be taught to everyone, Jew and gentile alike? Do you think that the gentile has a place in the correction process, or is this meant for study by Jews alone? And what is the correction process all about?**

A.3 You may have read in the Bible that at the end of the correction all will know God, from the youngest to the eldest, with no regard to gender or race. The Kabbalah is about man and the desire to receive, which God created. All creatures have this desire to receive. Therefore, all who want to participate in the process of correction may do so. The correction is a process of exchanging one's intentions from egoistic to altruistic ones, i.e., from the benefit of oneself to the benefit of the Creator. It is hoped that all mankind will be involved in this process.

Q.4 **I am interested in learning more about Kabbalah. Isn't it essential for a beginning student like myself to first study the Bible, the written and the oral law for many years, before I begin learning Kabbalah, or can I start now?**

A.4 There are no prerequisite conditions to studying Kabbalah. All that is needed is one's curiosity and the will to learn. Through the study of Kabbalah one learns how to be similar to the spiritual world in one's deeds and thoughts.

Q.5 **I have heard rumors that a rabbi or Kabbalah student put a spell on someone so he would die. My questions: Is such a thing possible? And if so, is there a spell that can be said?**

Also, I have purchased several books related to "good" magical practices and would like to know if you can steer me in the right direction as far as some of these books go.

A.5 I do not know what books you have bought, but they do not deal with the true Kabbalah. Kabbalah is not about magic. Through study and reading you can gain a better understanding of Kabbalah. We recommend several types of readings, e.g., the articles we prepare in which we teach about the stages of man's development along his spiritual course. While it is important to study with a teacher and in a group setting, you can access these articles through our Web site, and special prayer books that we produce.

Q.6 **Seven years ago, I began my search for God, the Creator, the Father. Along the way my entire life was destroyed and I lost everything I held dear. One day I told Him, "I will not give up until you answer me! You are all I have left." Now I have begun to experience lights around people and animals. Isn't this a manifestation of Kabbalah? I want to know God and to develop spiritually.**

A.6 Your situation is precisely what motivates man to study Kabbalah. The way to know God is very difficult and requires specific study. And only after a spiritual feeling becomes revealed to him, does a man understand that his former feelings were just products of his imagination. One cannot feel God until he ascends to the upper worlds by turning all his egoistic characteristics into altruistic ones.

Q.7 **I understand that the word Kabbalah is from the Hebrew verb *lekabbel*, to receive. What does this mean and what is the purpose of receiving?**

A.7 In the beginning, the Creator alone existed. He created a general desire to receive. This desire to receive is called The First Man (*Adam HaRishon*). In order to enable The First Man to communicate with the Creator, the general desire to receive has been divided into many parts. The purpose of the creation is to achieve communion with the Creator, because only in such a state can man achieve fulfillment, endless tranquility and happiness.

Q.8 Does this imply that at some time in the distant future, there will be only one man, again?

A.8 The Kabbalah does not deal with our physical body, but only with our spiritual component. The upper world is like one creature, one soul whose parts are projected to a lower world (the one we perceive) in which we feel ourselves as distinct from each other. To explain this more simply: Because we are limited within our egoism, we feel ourselves as separated from each other, despite the fact that we are all of us actually one spiritual body. Therefore, the separation exists only within our mistaken perception, for we are all in fact one.

Q.9 What are some of the concepts I will find in The Zohar? And who wrote The Zohar?

A.9 The book of The Zohar explains how a man in this world can reach the source of his soul. This road, or ladder, consists of 125 steps. The author of The Zohar must have passed through all of these stages. The soul of Rabbi Yehuda Ashlag had reached the same heights (and spiritual place) as the author of The Zohar, Rabbi Shimon Bar Yochai. This is why Baal HaSulam was able to complete the commentary on The Zohar, which we can use today.

Q.10 Are you affiliated with other rabbis and other Kabbalah centers?

A.10 Bnei Baruch is not connected in any manner to any other groups or organizations that deal with Kabbalah.

Q.11 Do you have a list of books or study materials that you could send me in English, French or Spanish?

A.11 Unfortunately, there are no reputable, serious Kabbalah books written in any language other than Hebrew and Aramaic and based on authentic sources, i.e., Shimon Bar Yochai, the Ari, Yehuda Ashlag, etc. Bnei Baruch has created a basic course in Kabbalah through its Web site, and is publishing books for beginners in several languages, including Spanish, German and Russian. The latest publication by Bnei Baruch, *Attaining the Worlds Beyond,* is available in English and Russian.

Q.12 I was raised in a religion other than Judaism. It is my belief there are more gods, more holy spirits, etc., than are mentioned in Kabbalah. And isn't the purpose of creation to give man a better life in this world, as well as the world to come? I look around me and see what a terrible place this world can be.

A.12 There exists only the Creator and man. The purpose of creation is to ascend to the upper worlds while being in this world. This can be done if man's thoughts and desires are equivalent to the desires and thoughts of the upper worlds, a subject taught in Kabbalah. One who wants to ascend and reach the goal of creation (which is each man's personal goal in life, or he must return to this world after his death) must think positively about all creation.

Q.13 I am beginning to understand that I must take responsibility for my own actions, my own ego. I want to attain a more spiritual level in my life. Where do I start? And if I study Kabbalah, will I be able to act freely?

A.13 Man must always imagine that he stands in front of God, the Super Power. Everyone who studies Kabbalah and rises to a certain spiritual level can acquire such capabilities from this Super Power that allow him to use them as he wishes. And the greater his spiritual level, the more Creator-like characteristics and powers the Kabbalist achieves. Because of this, we may also say that the Kabbalist is able to act as freely and independently as the Creator. But no true Kabbalist will ever share these intimate experiences with others.

Q.14 I read somewhere that there is a portion of the Kabbalah that contains the 72 words or names for God and when read, the scripture makes known a message. Also, when the Hebrew characters are viewed vertically, they appear in columns of three characters and each column contains a word for God. I don't know if you ever noticed that God hides things in plain view, as is the case here.

A.14 Kabbalah utilizes many mathematical concepts such as matrices, geometry, numbers, graphs, characters and letters, etc. These approaches are codes, shown in the Bible, which inform us of spiritual objects and the connection between them. Each spiritual level has its own name or number equivalent based on the sum of all letters in the name. The transformation of a name to a number is called gematria. These codes refer to spiritual levels that we should attain.

Q.15 I live in London. I am not Jewish but over the past few years I have become interested in Kabbalah and have also developed an increasing, personal interest in Judaism. Are you able to provide any guidance whereby I can increase my knowledge? Do you have any representatives/members in the U.K. whom it would be possible to meet?

A.15 There are no Kabbalists of repute living outside of Israel. However, we recommend that you begin to study, access our web site, and send us questions and requests.

Q.16 **The Kabbalah seems to have ideas similar to all the major mystical traditions, such as Buddhism. Is there an important difference? If so, why should one choose this way and not another? If there is not, why isn't it acknowledged by Kabbalists?**

A.16 The general idea of all religious and mystical teachings is to commune with an upper entity. Every person comes with his own reason for seeking communion with this entity. For example, some people wish to enjoy an enriched and happy life in this world, to merit prosperity, health, confidence, a better future. They want to understand this world as much as possible in order to better manage their lives. Others wish to learn how to manage in the world to come after death. All of these goals are selfish and arise from man's egoism.

Kabbalah does not deal at all with these reasonings. Rather, Kabbalah aims to change man's nature in order to enable him to have qualities similar to those of the Creator.

The Kabbalistic method states that man must use everything he has in this world with the intention of giving to the Creator. To reach this intention, however, man needs to sense the Creator and must feel that the Creator enjoys his deeds. One who studies Kabbalah begins to understand its meaning through the sensing of the Creator.

Other Books by
Rabbi Michael Laitman

A Guide to the Hidden Wisdom of Kabbalah with Ten Complete Kabbalah Lessons provides the reader with a solid foundation for understanding the role of Kabbalah in our world. The content was designed to allow individuals all over the world to begin traversing the initial stages of spiritual ascent toward the apprehension of the upper realms.

Attaining the Worlds Beyond is a first step toward discovering the ultimate fulfillment of spiritual ascent in our lifetime. This book reaches out to all those who are searching for answers, who are seeking a logical and reliable way to understand the world's phenomena. This magnificent introduction to the wisdom of Kabbalah provides a new kind of awareness that enlightens the mind, invigorates the heart, and moves the reader to the depths of their soul.

About Bnei Baruch

Bnei Baruch is a non-commercial group that is spreading the wisdom of Kabbalah to accelerate the spirituality of mankind. This mission is mainly achieved through free Kabbalah classes that are provided throughout Israel, the ongoing maintenance of a very large Web site in twenty languages, and the production of a wide variety of publications that are distributed on a not-for-profit basis. The core group is made up of approximately 140 families, who each contribute part of their earnings toward maintaining a central learning center in Israel. All members of the core group hold regular jobs or own businesses. Collective activities include weekend and holiday meals, and the men gathering for three hours before the break of dawn every morning to conduct intensive Kabbalah studies. Thousands of people around the world access these live sessions on the Internet, and participate in daily Kabbalah discussions through online forums. In addition to the round-the-clock efforts of the members of the group and their families, Bnei Baruch's students throughout Israel and the world perform a wide variety of tasks associated with spreading the wisdom of Kabbalah on a voluntary basis.

In recent years, a massive, worldwide search for the answers to life's questions has been underway. Society has lost its ability to see reality for what it is and in its place easily formed viewpoints and opinions have appeared. Bnei Baruch reaches out to all those who are seeking awareness beyond the standard, to people who are seeking to understand what our true purpose for being here is. Bnei Baruch offers practical guidance and an extremely rewarding way of life for those searching for a logical and reliable method of understanding the world's phenomena.

How to Contact Bnei Baruch

Bnei Baruch
P.O. Box 584,
Bnei Brak 51104 Israel
Fax: +972-3-5781795

E-mail address: info@kabbalah.info
Web site: www.kabbalah.info

Toll free in Canada and USA:
1-866-LAITMAN